Mocambo Nights:
Poetry from the Mocambopo
Reading Series

MoCaMBo NiGHts

PoetRY FRoM tHe MoCaMBoPo PoetRY ReaDInG SeRIes

EDiteD BY
PatRICK Lane

Ekstasis  Editions

National Cataloguing in Publication Data
Lane, Patrick (Ed.)
      Macombo nights: Poems from the Macombopo Reading Series.
      Poems
      ISBN 1-896860-90-7

1. Canadian poetry (English)--British Columbia--Victoria.* 2. Canadian poetry (English)--20th century.* I. Lane, Patrick, 1939- II. Mocambo Cafe.
PS8295.7.V52M62 2001   C811'.5408'0971128   C2001-910874-5
PR9198.3.V52M62 2001

Cover Art: Miles Lowry

Acknowledgments
We would like to thank Yvonne Blomer and Sara Selecky for their untiring work in helping to assemble this anthology. As well we would like to thank John and Claire Yoo, who provide the space at Mocambo to us every Friday night. And Carla Biagioni who works behind the counter with a ready smile, many thanks, and to Amanda Butler, before her, who had a great ear for great poetry. "Voula," by Karen Connelly is from *The Disorder of Love* (Gutter Press); "Were You to Die" Steven Heighton is from *The Ecstasy of Skeptics* (House of Anansi); "The Owl and The Mouse" by Susan McCaslin is from *The Altering Eye* (Borealis Press); "Titanic"by John Pass *The Water Stair* (Oolichan Press); "The Fourth Moon of Broadway" by Ron Smith is from *Enchantment and Other Demons* (Oolichan Books); "Family History" by Susan Stenson is from *Could Love a Man* (Sono Nis Press).

Published in 2001 by:
Ekstasis Editions Canada Ltd.   Ekstasis Editions
Box 8474, Main Postal Outlet   Box 571
Victoria, B.C. V8W 3S1   Banff, Alberta T0L 0C0

LE CONSEIL DES ARTS | THE CANADA COUNCIL
DU CANADA | FOR THE ARTS
DEPUIS 1957 | SINCE 1957

BRITISH
COLUMBIA
ARTS COUNCIL
Supported by the Province of British Columbia

Mocambo Nights has been published with the assistance of a grant from the Canada Council and the Cultural Services Branch of British Columbia.

Contents

Foreword

There's always a place for poets to meet and read. When I was young back in the Sixties it was The Advance Mattress Coffee House in Vancouver. Earle Birney, Dorothy Livesay, Milton Acorn, and bill bissett were just a few of the regulars who read poetry there. For Gwendolyn MacEwen and Margaret Atwood it was The Bohemian Embassy in Toronto. New poems slid along the walls and nestled among the flickering candles at the tables where artists and academics, workers and wanderers nodded their approval to a good line or a stunning image. The Mocambo Café is the place in Victoria. Every Friday night for years writers have gathered there to hear poetry.

Wendy Morton, the indomitable host of the reading series, is the one who arranges for writers to come in from across the country with grants from the Canada Council for the Arts and the League of Canadian Poets, but also, and just as importantly, provides a place for the unknown, the nearly-known, the almost-but-not-quite-well-known new writers to show their stuff at the open mike. They're the ones who make the Friday nights shine and they're the ones who come as regulars to laugh or sit silently in intense quiet listening to a poem that is so awesome it shivers the mind.

Young writers from the University of Victoria wander down to jostle shoulders and read at the open mike with street poets, spoken word poets, and performance poets from around the city. Writers drift in from Vancouver to listen and read there. Brand-new writers just out of high school or off the street in Vanderhoof, Nanaimo, Tsawwassen, Grande Prairie, Swift Current, The Pas, or wherever in Canada, arrive in Victoria ready to begin their lives as poets. They get a room somewhere downtown or crash with a new friend and start talking poetry. They ask of each other the old question, "Where's it happening?" "Who's reading?"

The name of Mocambo Friday nights comes up immediately. Atwood and MacEwen, bissett, Acorn and myself once sat at similar tables and waited for our turn to read and perform. It's been like this for centuries in cultures all over the world, from China to England and from France to Russia. It's how writers get started. It's how they find an audience and measure themselves against a present and a past.

This anthology, Mocambo Nights, is a collection of poets who've read at the coffee house over the years. The book is Wendy Morton's idea. She asked me to edit it and I was happy to do it. Collections like this are what makes poetry happen. They document a time, a place, and a generation.

The reading series was started in 1995 by Jim Andrews, who gave it the name Mocambopo. Tanya Kern then took over as host, then Seth Gotro and in 1999, Wendy Morton became the host. And so it's gone, every Friday night for 6 years. The owners of the coffee house are John and Claire Yoo. They have to be thanked for providing the space, the coffee, and the friendly, easy-going atmosphere that is a Mocambo night.

Mocambo Nights comes out of Victoria, a small city on an island in the far west, but this book's presence will be felt across the country. Inside these covers are new and exciting poems by every poet you can imagine and some you couldn't possibly imagine. The range of voices is broad. Poets from across the country appear at The Mocambo Café to read from new work and old. Established writers like Don McKay, Lorna Crozier, Brian Brett, Karen Connelly, Patrick Friesen, Patricia and Terence Young, Pete Trower, and Tim Lilburn share the coffee house with new and startling writers like Margo Button, Susan Gee, Robert Gore, Jolene Heathcote, Marlene Grand-Maitre, Susan Stenson, and Leanne McIntosh. Poems by these many writers take in the whole spectrum and they will take you in too if you let them.

Here in Mocambo Nights is a taste of what is happening right now in poetry. When you read a poem that makes you laugh or makes you cry, then read on a bit further. After you're done, slip on your shoes and head down to the Mocambo Café. Wendy's the one introducing everyone. She's the one who gives out the prizes at the end of the night. And the coffee, the cold drinks, and the tea? Well, they're just like the poetry, the best in town.

Patrick Lane

MOCAMBO NIGHTS

Laurie Abel

Three Women Smoking

The women come to the ocean
purses strapped over their shoulders,
they sit on rocks, smoke cigarettes,
talk about last night

about that son of a bitch
who didn't come home; about
when they were teenagers
about...

Hard women who
if you ask them,
will trace the family tree
to a murderer, but say
he was adopted and so
not really in the blood.

What's in my blood?
That I fall hard
for men who do not want to love.

My grandmother told me
get married, have children.
        Soon. She had two,
but mothered thirteen siblings
and every hard-luck niece and nephew.

At her kitchen table, she'd tell me stories,
her cigarettes burning down
on Ray's drinking. Drink?
Like a fish. That time at
Rice Lake...

Grandmother, I was wondering
if you could understand
37 and still no children. If you
could understand walking by
the ocean, and wanting to join
these women smoking.

Mark Conrad Asser

Direct Action

Shaking bones,
Snake eyes rattle against white knuckles,
Dreams in ivory are spun to the table top.
A fortune to be willed or crapped out
By the stars on the edge of a cube.

Shaking bones,
Chicken toes and Baboon teeth cupped in a worn palm.
Queequak killers are dropped in to the dust.
A future foretold or denied
By the mandala between the haunches.

Shaking bones,
A sliver of saint's shin inlaid in worn stone
Ancient relics polished by hesitant lips
A soul is fortified or dammed
By the whispers of the faithful.

Shaking bones,
Fist clenched around a buffalo thigh
Hard and white the bloodied bone
Brought down to change the future.

Where is my brother?
There!
Bones shaking.

Clive Beal

Liberty

names of nonverbal reasoning
smells of woodsmoke
deep in memory smells

evocative colours resound
once remembered, down
below ocean swells

of the sea of memory
deep where wistful dwells
the mystic seahorse personality
now bleached like the coral
of the shallow, too warm sea

Remember the war
remember how to get the answer
if you don't remember the answer, itself
remember the ancestors
and forgive them our loss
and remember small joy
whatever the cost

all around the sound of memory
speechless tone poems cast
like the tolling that cracks the bell:
the first ring is the last.

Lindsay Beal

Grendel, dreaming

She grows from
dandelion, ginger, licorice
roots.

Her breath the musky steam of
an earth oven fire pit.
With cinnamon bark
and mulled wine,
she dreams
milk showers—

The Grendel girl remembers mother
and suckling sister, nestled;
the cool one, cradled, grows from
milk weed, thistledown, dandelion
seeds.

Grendel from the
bitter root
hot root
sweet root
punctured with thistle thorns
planted with seeds
sprouting cool milk dreams
of someone she could
never be.

bill bissett

wuns i saw it raining frogs

it was sumwher neer salmo
in th southern kootenees   was
getting a ride in an old
packard   creekee n th lites
sort uv shining thru th rain

slurp slurp n creek creek   he
didint take much notis uv th
frogs   iuv nevr seen it rain
cats n dogs but frogs   ther
wer frogs evree wher plop plump

on th soft shouldr   guttrs n
croak croak   it was hard to
tell from how far up they wer
dropping on account uv th

thickness uv th rain nd th
frogs themselvs   he didint seem
to take anee speshul notis uv
kept on driving   staring ahed i
think heud seen ths bfor   sure

is a wet wun he sd peering past
th wind shield wiprs th rain n
th frogs falling on th hood   yes
i sd   its like raining cats n

dogs   he turnd n lookd at me
sharp   concernd abt me   coz
aneewun cud tell it was frogs

falling heer

Yvonne Blomer

Through the Temple With Buddha

On cool afternoons
while my students eat lunch
I slip out
down the street
enter the quiet cemetery
and bow low
shyly, for fear of offending.
You step down
from that high post
and stand beside me.
We fall into a comfortable stride
while you talk
of the people who dwell
in this ancient house of yours.
The woman
killed by her husband
at 22
for bearing 2 daughters
no sons.
2 daughters already
and only 22.
A child curled
in the dry curve
of each arm
hungry infants.
And the men
hundreds of them
who died in the coal mines
lives lived by the light
of ancient candles.
These walks
are fantasies
in your mind.

I come every day
bow low
shy
you open your eyes
to watch
uncertain of who I am
a pale blonde
blue eyed stranger.
You want to teach
your timeless patience
to trust
this soft face
un-powdered
but white
as the bones in the graves
you guard.

Brian Brett

The Tourists Ascend Dragon Gate Pass

Poling up the gorge,
the old bargeman leaning on
his spiked bamboo rod

knows all the ancient ballads—
        Ho, divine river.
        Ho, hear my song.
        Ho, hear it again
for I am old and worship your water.

        The passengers are bored.
They've already bought enough trinkets,
        and the river is long. A gaunt
boy living in the hovel gouged into the mountain
        runs along the riverbank,
and the tourists from Chongqing amuse themselves,
throwing Yuan notes into the torrent,
watching them float past
        the little boy
too scared to dive into the icy water,
following, like a sandpiper on the shore,
        the course of lost
money in the emerald rapids.

Timothy Brownlow

What is poetry?

Houseman didn't dare shave thinking of it,
Dickinson felt like it was eternal
Cold or the top of your head coming off.

It's what gets lost in translation, the créme
De la créme, primal, unreasonable;
Like freedom, in constant need of defence.

Impossible to define. Without it
All definitions would lose precision,
All dictionaries not worth swallowing.

Emanating a kind of chlorophyll
Keeping tolerable the air we breathe.
Each poet magnifies the sacred grove:

Listen to the voice of those wind-swept woods.

The trees remain, the planters disappear.

The storied land

"...such as she would become." Robert Frost

The soil tilled is soft and light, little range
straight along a string stretched from stake to brick.
The garden is a bar code sprouting line
by line, leaves, stems and roots we'll wash and eat.
Beyond the garden edge the forest greens
around a single apple tree, mummied fruit
still on the branch, twigs snowy with blossoms.
Once, a boy put paper Indians on the house's
ground floor windows, to keep the wild
animals from coming in at night. Now,
we've less cause for fancy: last winter,
one turkey at the feeder, three times, one fox.
And today, a pair of bluebirds came through.
We watch them from inside; we hope they stay.

Margo Button

The Dead Have Birthdays

Your thirtieth birthday, I daydream
you come home for the day,
returned from a long northern voyage.
You are strong and tall again, your old self.
I told you I'd be back, you say
with the same crooked grin, warm embrace.
Where I have been
there is no word for good-bye.

You're a man now with a certain reticence,
the woman you love at your side —
This is the one, Mom, you whisper.
She's Inuit. I imagine
your children — black eyes, blond curls.

You'll tell them bedtime stories
of ling cod you speared in Schooner Cove
as a boy — the gleaming green flesh.
Summers you fished off Cape Scott,
gutted hundreds of salmon, each silver body
coating you with its armour.
A two hundred pound halibut
took three of you to pull in.
You never forgot the astonished eyes
staring from one side of its head.

Today, you bring us Arctic char.
I've baked a chocolate cake
with thirty candles that won't blow out.
We give you a dictionary of Inuinnaqtun.
Quana, you say, Quanapiaqutin.
You have a model qayak for your dad,
a book for me about Iqaluit women
who carve their lives out of soapstone.

So many adventures to tell —
skidooing at night across Elu Inlet
you heard the dancing green sky speak
the crackling tongues of snow.
You passed by Inuit hunters who sit
for hours hunkered over a hole in the ice
waiting for a seal to come up for air.
Quinuituq, they call it there —
deep patience.

Sara Cassidy

in the kitchen of forgetting

the kettles have boiled dry
and the fridge self-defrosts

the herbs in the garden outside the door
have long been used —
      first, the cook took all the leaves
then, the stems
then, chopped at the roots
and still boils a teaspoon of the dirt
when hope seizes her

the cookbooks are written with lemon juice
and there is no fire left, no gas for the stove

the carrot peeler has peeled
every carrot to its very very centre
the meat tenderizer has gone soft

in its drawer
the cutlery has dulled until
knife is indistinguishable
from spoon from fork
your hand would do just as well

the kitchen sink is most absent
a wedding ring down its drain

all meals are served in colanders

the dinner bell is hungry,
                                its tongue dry
it wants you to come to the table
and tell about your day

you are cutting through a field
                stile to stile
the cows raise their heavy heads to you
        and blink their large blank eyes

on the wall of the kitchen of forgetting
is a calendar with a picture of a farm
that has been faded by the sun sifted
through the screen door

in the picture a woman
holds her skirt close
as she steps over a stone wall

Karen Connelly

Voula

Rebetiko is a hypnotic, passionate style of music and dance which became popular in Greece in the 1930's and '40's. It was, and still is, the music of the poor and of social outcasts, similar in many ways to Gypsy Flamenco. Traditionally it is played and danced only by men.

Little spot

is the meaning of my name,
but look at me, my life
is big as the sun, I am Voula,
I am famous.

"She is ugly," they'll tell you,
"a dirty-dog woman, a junky
covered in sores
and a bitch besides,"

but look at my young lovers,
tekna-mou,
Sonia from Brazil,
Katerina from the north,
Sinead from Ireland with
all her silk and lace.

I am Voula
I am famous.

If you see me dance rebetiko
you too will love me,
you will watch and look away
with burning eyes.
Even Vaso's plates know
the disorder of love, they leap
off the tables and shatter
just to touch my feet.

With these scuffed boots
I sway hard and slow inside
the music, my arms in the air,
elbows crooked above my head:
I am balancing each star high
above the plane trees.

Lorna Crozier

The End of the Century

Under the bridge the dead are gathering.
What happened to the ferryman, his bag
of coins, his pity? In all this traffic
how can they cross these girders of steel
and starlight? One of them hears a creaking.
It is you in your father's rowboat,
newly painted. Your lunch beside you
on the seat, in the bow that singer
who died young. He has spelled you
on this journey but now he begins
in Mandarin the version of Red River
he learned in exile in the fields
far from Beijing. Under the bridge,
hearing him, the dead, too, start singing
We will miss your bright eyes
and sweet smile, in at least
a dozen different tongues.

Prayer

I don't know why I
imagine you sad. I've spent the day

divining ivy & lavender, tracing
sunlight as it glances off slant

of walls, dishes as I wash them, cups
& bowls transparent

in my hands. I don't know if
sorrow is yours, or mine

or everyone's in some kind of strange
convergence. In the evening I visit

the jewish cemetery at the top of the hill
where two roads meet, wanting

the stillness of spirits, stones laid upon
graves to signify a presence remembered,

to signify love. Someday my bones will make silt
with the earth, or ashes of my flesh be cast

to sea at sunset. It is said there is memory
in the cells of our own bodies, so I do

not know which burial to choose.

You tell me you are happy.

I will not question this.

Mike Doyle

Picking Blackberries

That one time, over by Uplands Park in hot August sun,
carrying the rake for hooking, prising apart
tangles of bushy undergrowth, longhandled
clippers for clearing the way, blackberry-stained
gardening gloves, a seam of the right thumb
come unstitched, and the plastic ice-cream bucket
filling all too slowly, for others had been before us.

Many of the halfhidden clumps and clusters
pale and hard still, mostly I stuck to the task,
concentrating on lifting knots of berries,
fingering them softly off the branches
one by one, into the bottomless bucket,
a seventy-year-old along with his partner,
working companions, together for a quiet
industrious hour. That one time I looked up
to see her, again, arms uplifted to the laden
tendrils; for an instant her gaze directed
towards me in familiar invitation.

Forty years beyond this life yet still
she gestures to me, smiling slightly,
still I see the moment in which I am frozen
and still am frozen in my failure to answer.

Today at last I can feel my bucket filling;
if I could touch her just once more I should gently
in one sure movement put a blackberry
to her parting lips, and watch the red stain spreading,
life beginning to flow again, affirming:
Yes. Yes. Yes. The blood of being.

Clearing 1

late afternoon sun blazes off birch trees and I'm caught by a clearing
       where I was born
I know that light like I know the wind that spoke and speaks light as
       linen on a line
I remember how the mind moved rustling like a small animal in
       underbrush skittering among the leaves

there is room for sadness here this is the place where a boy under
       stands more than he knows
barbed wire and wild roses the tangle of a man's life how he
       encounters himself looking back
an old hand on the bark of a poplar his eyes still wondering at the
       fish lurking in the creek

you know how it works how you have to stand still letting the light
       climb up your trunk
you have to forget most things human this is not a place where any
       thing has happened
you are a man I don't know how else to say it you are a man who
       has always sought god

there is a kind of indifference here hushed and slow it doesn't matter
       when you go
it doesn't matter what you know you are always a child here neither
       lost nor found not making strange
there is nothing you owe but the words you come to and those
       words are your seal

there is room for a mind between the high prairie sky and this
       scrappy undergrowth
how the air stirs shifting from one silence to another something
       about to happen
bare thickets in the fall a last pale rain arriving the way distant
       thunder hollows out the afternoon

the boy learns to stand among the trees a kind of listening at the
        edge of things
it's the step in that kills the man released into the open helpless and
        abandoned
if it wasn't for the rain who could live through the clearing if it
        wasn't for that mercy?

Gary Geddes

What Does A House Want?

A house has no unreasonable expectations
of travel or imperialist ambitions;
a house wants to stay
where it is

A house does not demonstrate
against partition or harbour
grievances;
                    a house is a safe
haven, anchorage, place
of rest

Shut the door on excuses
— greed, political expediency

A house remembers
its original inhabitants, ventures
comparisons:
                    the woman
tossing her hair
on a doorstep, the man
bent over his tools and patch
of garden

What does a house want?

Laughter, sounds
of love-making, to strengthen
the walls;
                    a house
wants people, a permit
to persevere

A house has no stones
to spare; no house has ever been convicted
of a felony, unless privacy
be considered a crime in the new
dispensation

What does a house want?

Firm joints, things on the level, water
rising in pipes

Put out the eyes, forbid
the drama of exits,
entrances; somewhere
in the rubble a mechanism
leaks time,
               no place
familiar for a fly
to land
on

Susan Gee

What we saw at the lake

When the heron flies
his wings fold down
feathers nearly touching
blue bits of water
soft sweep
he draws into himself
something
from the lake

we stretch
arms and legs through summer water
swimming to the reeds
going farther than most

on the shore
you give me new language
trace it over the palm of my hand
a secret hieroglyphic

I roll transparent shapes
into fluttering words
hoping for translation
You hold what I've said on the edges
of your body

you are long blue
heron feathered
sitting on the shore that slides away from us

far off
over the water
the heron leaves his perch
and you whisper
there is no life
without wings.

William George

Sockeye Salmon Dream

sockeye salmon dream
seeps into my bones flesh
the west coast rain sings

Robert Gore

A Largeness in the Air

When I think of nudes it's not Renoir, Matisse
not the man's approach hard at midnight
it's her mouth dripping blossom
and white, the secret smell her skin exhales.
      Tanya Kern

There is a largeness in the air, trees billow
into shapes of their own making,
spring airs out the willows into their green
laughter, their hair fills with birds singing
in major and minor keys. To follow
the way paint comes at the canvas and spills
over the edge of the ocean, blue so brilliant
it keeps the sky in place. I want to keep you
and I can't, scrub shapes from bowls of fruit so
when I think of nudes it's not Renoir, Matisse

but Chagall, a woman in a red dress
flying above the city, the cloth held against
her body with the cleft of wind that sounds
of midnight. A clock in the centre plants
the town down in its green hills, a stress
of notes gathers the cool air over the river,
shades of birds in the hollows
where their voice enters
the blue edge that scrapes the dawn,
not the man's approach hard at midnight

that strings us along into territory
we can't know for seeing, the eye caught out
with the first brush of how the painter stills
the flesh, a waxen flower caught and fondled
in the wash of some unexpected
walled and varnished dream, brown earth
leaking from the frame into each aqua,
each meridian of long desire. The door opening
into a pulse of silence where
it's her mouth dripping blossom

that he can't contain, no way to touch
and keep compact the aureole of her own
green life, keys are constant in the list
of old and textured music that tones and tongues
and keeps him at his paints, colours are a trap
that catch him, windows open on a light
that airs him out each spring, though this year
he's lost heart and the town falls down
around the feet of mapmakers, black
and white, the secret smell her skin exhales.

Marlene Grand Maitre

Waiting In The House On Harwood

This Spring, iris leaves are a green
that defies loss, shaped
like the fingers of those who died
too early, reaching back
for what they left unfinished.
My father, dead at thirty-two, left
a four year old daughter
waiting in the house on Harwood.

Forty years later, cleaning
mother's basement after her heart attack,
I find his wallet, black leather,
still holding the curve of his left hip.
Tucked inside, a dry cleaning ticket
from Nelson's on Cambie, dated for pick-up
the day after his death.
Probably his wedding suit, the only one
a welder needed then, the grey worsted

he'll be wearing if I look down now,
my bare feet standing on his dress shoes.
He is teaching me to waltz
one two three, one two three,
he sets me on the floor, tells me
to watch then twirls an imaginary partner,
gliding out of sight.

XLII

Simplicity in play
as Wilfred Mellers wrote
about Bellini's style
creates fresh subtleties.
Such work is lyrical.
Each tiny change sets off
a vast harmonic web
in one's accompaniment
establishing new links
so work completes itself
in novel nuances.
You learn to give notes space
as Monk so quickly learned
so these can integrate
such feelings in the soul
where thought is intimate.

Roy Green

Honeycomb Bull's Eye

There are many bees living in my heart

Transforming my failure into honey

Honey golden translucent in the hive

Busy all the time like Jackson Pollock

Anointing his canvas with shooting stars

I shake like a wineglass in an earthquake

I offer you a portrait of my dog

Nostalgia rebels against the present

I present to you a quivering place

Pregnant with charisma and plump fried fish

I'll burn bright red candles, Friday for sure

Attracting with quarks and charmed particles

The quivering space of Cupid's pleasure

It's whispering words inside of your mouth

Vivian Hansen

Tunnelling

I have learned so much
inside tunnels.
The three clovers of Roger's Pass
through which I drove
with a man I married
but never mated.
The black pitch of false night
scaring us around unsure turns,
and glass eyes: predatory cars gliding toward us
       threatening.

Years later, minus the man,
a London Tube hurtles me through time.
I see Roman aqueducts clean
beneath modern London
in a thousand years
brick and mortar still solid.

the rising duct-curls
distract me from the Moslem woman
who begs soundlessly, coins for
her glass eyes clouded with shame.

In the tunnels of Toronto
connecting,
you and I
losing the eyes of men,
into words   we pull underground.

I marvel at the white thoughts
            of your backbone
sliding against my fingers
and your cat-like lean
into my hip
as I follow your liquid eyes
into grotto.

Joelene Heathcote

Temporary Wives

Everyone knew the sound of your name Han Sung,
blooming in the honey ether of late morning. No other
name could take its place. Han Sung, the neighbourhood wives
are leaning out their windows, their faces are filling with light.
They hear everything. When I call your name like this,
these wives dream of your skin, the melon-scent of you,
smooth and flawless as desert.
Han Sung, how long we wait for someone
to bring an end to our loving,
for something this pure refuses secrecy.

                  The light is pulling back
from the floor like a golden train,
leaving us trembling. The house wives are sobbing
for you Han Sung, your dark mouth loving me,
potent as 1 Insam, illicit as 2 Potion Tong, for your
eyes that are lost in me, in the impossible distance
between you and the oasis of my flesh.

                  After love we stand by the window
to let our bodies cool and watch the dragonflies
mating, their shelled bodies meeting
in the stroboscopic purr of wings,
until so much appetite turns the sky dark
and you turn away from me.

Dinners of salt fish and corn tea are growing cold
in the kitchens of the house wives. They are waiting
for their husbands to return, Han Sung. They are waiting
for you, for other afternoons like this
where the scent of you lingers in the corridor, in the linen
they have hung in the sunshine, where your lips
open their hearts. But evening comes too soon,
and you disappoint them when you leave —
crossing the parking lot just as their eyes gently close.

         There is no other way for us.
You drive your long, gold car to the airport for me,
bow tenderly as the plane leaves the ground, and I stop breathing.
You fight traffic back to the office.
         The house wives will draw the blinds
when immigration comes looking for me.
They will shake their delicate heads
when they see the photographs of your dark skin on me,
the ones taken by the gardener
when you thought we'd gone unnoticed. They cannot
blame me for giving myself to you. They too have.
And their mouths Han Sung, their beautiful mouths
will fill as mine does, with the sound of your name, heavy
when they least expect it. They will carry this with them—
the sweet burden of you, hiding it from their husbands
like a pregnancy, an arraignment Han Sung
that has ruined them for other men.

Steven Heighton

Were You to Die

Were you to die I'd be free to go off
and see the world, and sleep in every elsewhere
I might never arrive
— yet I might choose to travel alone
from window to window looking out
on the streets of your city
where your friends still expect to see you sometimes
or mistake you for someone, out of custom — love —

Without your thrashing, manic dreams, my body
would sleep better
but wake more tired, I'd let the garden go to seed
the way I always meant to
and when I looked out the window into the yard
I'd never miss the snowpeas, beets and roses
but your sunhat I might miss — you hunkered down
in a summer dress, your fingers
grouped like roots in the raised beds,
your stooped, stubborn nape, your cinnamon-
freckled shoulders —

Were you to die, my heart
would be free to pack a bag
and book passage for the riot of islands
I might have been, and shared
with the one and numberless "beloved" we fumble
our whole lives glimpsing
a moment too late
when Eden was always the one who stayed
rooted in her changes, and gave you
the island in her arms, and when you slept
somehow she travelled, and when you woke
she was changed —

Were you to die, my mind
would be free to twist inward
the way fingers fist, and fasten pat
on its own taut notions, theorems, palm shut fast
to the snow that pooled there and seemed to flow through
when the skin still flowered in fullest winter
and I loved you, and thoughts, like books,
were doors that opened outward,
not coffins, closed,
not cells —

Were you to die and free me
my body would follow you down into the cold
prison of your passing, and warm you when all the others
had turned away, and try
bribing the keeper with a poem, or fool him
with keychains of chiming words — an elegy
so pure he'd be pressed to cry, eyes
thawing and the earth warmed, April
when rain falls like a ransom, through opened arms
that bore the sun down with you, warm.

Andreas Jensen

An Ancient Sea

I must go down to the seas again, for the call of the running tide
Is a wild call and a clear call that may not be denied;
And all I ask is a windy day with the white clouds flying,
And the flung spray and the blown spume, and the sea-gulls crying.
    John Masefield

It's easy for me living here, to walk the water's edge,
foot the cold pacific shores, stepping over grounded logs,
ducking sea-wash on a graveled windblown shore,
but it's the ancient prairie sea of grass that calls to me,
a hot wind on a hot day that stirs the foxtail heads to tossing,
the skree-ee of a hunting hawk high above a golden hillside,
and the smell of poplar trees and silver sage,
red willow in the sun by waters' edge.
But through all that, a nagging tumult checks me in mid-stride
I must go down to the seas again, for the call of the running tide

The call of the running rivers should be enough for me,
and the sough of the prairie wind in silverweed and sedge.
When did I last see, in wanton winter's morning beams
a coyote, solitary sentinel in a snow-decked pasture,
the sun-glow golden on his tawny flank?
Or at night, saw drifting across a silvan roadside
by the light of flaming skies, shadows that conspire
to take their places like a brown robed choir.
The song they sing, as they crouch round, side by side
Is a wild call and a clear call that may not be denied;

In spring, chinook winds blow the snow away,
the crocus races into bloom, puts the lie to worn out winter.
When thaw of spring touches deep inside each prairie creature,
and tells them the fearful times are nearly done, I must go
to a prairie slough and test the ice so quickly thinning,
give one final loud hurrah for winter dying.

When robins exult, meadow larks trill their scales from grey fence
posts
and vees of show geese gabble out their route to northern coasts,
then, on some hillside blushed with bloom, you'll find me lying
And all I ask is a windy day with the white clouds flying.

When winds of summer blow across this brineless sea,
I hear ancient combers break upon these ancient beaches.
It cannot be Pacific Ocean shores that call me home,
those crested coastlines have a foreign feel.
My roots are in the Baltic, and this,   this inland sea
of 200 million years ago. So now I'm fondly eyeing
the road back to my home, like the gopher to his hole
How it stirs my blood, sustains my soul, and I won't
miss those wave-tossed reaches, the endless sighing
And the flung spray and the blown spume, and the seagulls crying

Philip C. Kelly

The Two-Bladed Fan

There are some that will flee at the eyes whites' first sight
and there's others will quake in their place on that night
but a few, too, will rise to their innermost height
to take arms at alarms ken they not that they can
this is the tale of the two-bladed fan.

In a whirl will a girl unfurl curl to a lad
for the moment of foment his show lent a cad
danced askance, aslant stance, pants a glance and glands glad
for the treasure of pleasures bought dear when one can
and the cost is not lost on the two-bladed fan.

Hours enough has the night to delight rowdy crowd
with the band booming on strong in song, long and loud
stacks of snacks, limitless dipped chip trips, licked lips wowed
coffee's brewed, choose your booze, soda bottle or can
this is the world of the two-bladed fan.

Tokes and stogies provoke smoky choke-holds among
watered eye, sinus dry, tarry-tubercled lung
ere the grey wraith-wrap withers away as it's flung
torn by torque of the blades of the props — if they can
or such is the hope of the two-bladed fan.

Now the five-bladed fan was supposed to disperse
via five fast-spun fingers the worst of it first
but its wicker-weave paddles caught naught and it burst
toiling foils spoiled, void solenoid coils broiled rattan
though its arms had more charms than the two-bladed fan.

Nay neither did four-bladed fan take the slack
though it wished to enlist to assist the attack
for its bulb was too bright for the booths at the back
it was parked without spark, fixed by flicked-switch nix ban
though it had twice the arms of the two-bladed fan.

Though the three-bladed fan took its duty to heart
though it pivoted steadily right from the start
with its trinity spin thinning thickness in part
still it needed, depleted, the least of its clan
and this as we know is the two-bladed fan.

With its hum and its wobble in slow-building speed
meagre two-bladed fan turned to meeting the need
sparse propeller dispeller swept swelter and weed
till its last rotor motor's iota it ran
till the proud dying gasp of the two-bladed fan.

Now for tennis a five-bladed fan is divine
and for summer's eve reads light the four-blade design
open windows where wind blows and three blades are fine
but to thresh air fresh best bless by brave blades your plan
this is the tale of the two-bladed fan.

Tanya Kern

Belief

I dreamed all art was pissing in a jar
brimmed full with crucifixes
and the crows mortgaged their feathers
to pay my rent.

William Knowles

The Misanthrope in Me

Today I threw the first punch,
cut off a lady in a mustang
only a block from home.
It was rude and dangerous,
but that's the way life is —
my life, anyway.

First elevator of the morning,
way overcrowded,
everyone impatient for
another day of the same old crap.
A woman's enameled fingertip
hovers over the CLOSE button,
two triangles threaten a vertical line
over a Santa Claus sleigh
of Braille blisters.

For a moment
the misanthrope in me
swells to exactly four feet by six,
everyone is crushed
into the corners but
when the doors open again
I've shrunk back to size
and I don't think anybody's
noticed.

Men call their machines
by female pronouns, but
I say my bike's a male, because
it goes between your legs,
you don't get into it like
a car or a ship.

Today I rode the Italian,
bought it cheap from a friend
on his way down. Spends
his nights on Ecstasy now,
spends his days in apathy. We
don't talk much anymore.

Not that I care either.
Damn those kids in Africa,
let them starve. I throw out
the junk mail too. I'm just
going to ride my bike today.
Maybe I'll care tomorrow.

Beth Kope

Conception Park Revisited

My father was a moon faced man
says the small girl at the end of my bed.
She wavers, first a fist, sharp and clear, then
bleeds into the hidden, the shadows,
bends where the moon's fingers fragment the room.
Her nose is too big for her face,
her eyes are wide, brown with gold flecks;
they could lighten later.

Yes, I know, I met him on the path,
I answer. She is heavier on my legs
than someone that young should weigh,
legs swinging, punctuating her words.
Her gibbous face shines with the waxing moon's pull.
She's waiting for her world's fabrication
waiting and biting her lip with waiting.
The blood starts to curl down her chin.

Was he a good man, did he tell funny stories?
she asks, and my hands reach to staunch the blood's
messy tracks; my hands reach my own wound.
It is a map between my legs, issue of our country,
re-shaping the boundaries, loosened by tidal phases.
It's her, it's him, it's a hymn to escape
and she slides up my body
nestles her head under my chin.

I am confined, it is so, she is her father's daughter.
Hemmed by her weight, our eyes lock in eclipse,
the moon between us translating a shadowed path across my cheek.
She leaves me with a leaf in my palm torn from along the path.
And blood that knows. Blood that remembers.

Timothy Stuart Lander

Halifax

Despite the insistency of the rain
rain in the street
and I gotta find a doorway
        to sleep in
a doorway
  or a park shelter
    but sleeping places
      eradicated from the city
except for cars of course
   they can sleep in the shelter
      for five bucks a night
while the people wander
  with their wet feet
the uneasy night away
  of the rain pocked streets
Aging men who do not wish
  to be confined by walls
knowing that we live
  under the weather, the stars
     the rainclouds
under the trees
  under whatever we carry with us
    a piece of cloth, a skin of plastic
    to throw between us and heaven
    to lift and shudder with the wind
Aging men
  with rough and woolly cheeks and chins
    sitting
      watching the weather
        with wet feet and smelly feet

no one writes poems much
  about our tribe
    we're not glamorous
      have no heroics
    we're not earth shakers
our tales are full of fart, fog and
unaccomplishment
the inadequacies of forty years
  of loving up and down
    the old love dance
and easier now to sit and watch
  the rain from some doorway
    in someone else's city.

Death

I think of death sometimes, my own and others.
Purdy told me the worst of it was having no one
you could tell the story to who was there, no one
to dispute, to say that wasn't it at all, no one
to laugh in the pure knowing of it. Memory. A poet
once said *it* was the strangest word we know.
Agree or not, lonely is when the story runs out,
old is when the people do.

Tim Lilburn

Seeing

Pacific frozen a hundred miles off Siberia;
behind this skinned rabbit rivers, names
that haven't eaten in weeks, their wormy dents
in snow, wolf-chewed bacilli,
the plane's shadow nervous on a green like
                                 a flowering cloud of forgetting,
then guttering down, becoming more and more physical, into China,
south of moony, atomic, living-in-its-stomach Harbin, Russian
                    clocktower and the giant scrubbed statue of Mao in
five o'clock coal haze, fields and first villages the inside of ropey bone.
The light is aging standing where it is.
Things move out of themselves everywhere, floaty, hulked
clots of nomads over north fields, the skin throws this off, traveling
under stars, the skin sweats this out a little, tree bark, cat tail,
sweating this out and the idea
is to get yourself taken in and rest a couple of nights in one
of the swaying wagons or travois, their smoky lamps and conversations
you don't understand going on while you try to sleep, hammocking over
                               the wave-tipped plain,
and suprisingly do sleep, waking holding a luminous apple like a hamster.
A herd of goats on the third day shows you
the magical, slightly frightening signs their hooves have made
in the sand around one of the camps.
Their bodies come out of their inner mouths, each gesture
        rimmed with gold, a small yellow bell
          ringing caught inside. They let you be for a moment
a turbulence in their eye as they look at you
but this makes the bubble in your head feel as if it were slipping and
you turn away. And they give you back, a roll of open-
handed foam from their one, light-repelling essence
that lives in a sunken tree nowhere near here
and moves too quickly in its mammoth fixity for smell.

Mark Lindenberg

Problem-Solving

Yesterday,
I contemplated
beta-blockers

and high-class hookers
aloud, for some
of the same
reasons.

Paddy McCallum

The Pioneer Graveyard at Nicola Lake

The small fence around your stone
slumps like a cowshed
as death re-enters, hammer in hand.

Even in dreams you could not
get through, meeting him
on the road at midnight
or by the sea
or the apple tree.

Some men have minds
like the west, a hard perpetual
tomorrow, they build
the church first
and never enter it.

He stood here, right here
and beat out the words of your name
with the chisel and mallet
his hands had become

to find what outside himself
resembled you

worn granite, folded arms
still protecting, down
this hundred years and more,
still more, your
winter daughter

ten days old.

Susan McCaslin

The Owl and the Mouse

She is dreaming she is a small creature
swift and fragile
locked to earth's giant bones
snug in long tunnels—
a plain gray field mouse.

Out of the hunting wind,
imperious swoop and wing-span,
terrible, wider-than-God face
beautiful brown-shadowed moon face
of the owl with her ruffled feathers
floating down nearer and nearer

where she, terrified and in love,
opens herself in a sacrifice of delirium
to the narrowing space between them.

wash day

in a dug-out dirt basement
a wringer washer and two metal tubs
one two rinse   one to carry

        even in winter
        clothes pinned on the line
        steam leaving their bodies   spirits
        rising in to cold   disappearing

towels brought back in   twisted
smelling of frost and hard as tree bark

        my mother's hands   red
        laid out
        shirts   socks   pants
        on the kitchen table

the frozen shapes we wore
their cold shells
melting on my skin

Leanne McIntosh

Work of Art

For Thelma

My aunt sits on a chair in the kitchen
painting her legs tawny. It is wartime and
silk stockings are rationed, besides
it is summer and too hot for stockings.
She knows she is the center of my attention
and runs the brush along the curve of her calf
pauses in the hollow at the back of her knee, stops
at a place a few inches above her hemline.
I'm ten years old and I think she is beautiful.
My aunt signs for me to lift my skirt.
She brushes my leg, one stroke.
The scent of mock orange sweetens the heat.
And when she says, lean back,
lean back,
I strike a pose, a slipper
tipped from the toe of one foot,
my leg wet gold in the afternoon light.
There is a happy stranger inside me,
a woman pampered in a scented bath.
Pastel breasts and hips
a promise.

Don McKay

Song for the Song of the Coyote

Moondogs, moondogs,
tell me the difference between tricks
and wisdom, hunting
and grieving.
I listen in the tent, my ear
to the ground. There is a land even
more bare than this one, without sage,
or prickly pear, or greasewood. A land
that can only wear its scars, every crater
etched. Riverless. Treeless. You sing to its thin
used-up light, yips and floated tremolos and screams,
sculpted barks like fastballs of packed
air. Echoes that articulate the buttes and coulees and dissolve
into the darkness, which is always listening.

Andrea McKenzie

A Lesson In Love

Love was something you made your parents believe
before you went to bed.

I made a boy chase me,
pedaling faster and faster
in the rain.
Splooshing his thin legs through puddles.
I laughed
and later he kissed me.

Love fell from my tongue,
just a word I had heard.
I drew heart-shaped lines
when I was nine. "I love you."
How his face flushed
and his eyes gaped
wide and strained, like dry egg whites.
I was too big for my body.

I haven't learned love.
Hands and lips.
He said love after denting my mattress
and licking my ear.
What did he love?
It was just a word that needed to be heard.
I said it back.
What was I saying?
I was too big for my body.

I said it back.

Chris McPherson

What's left which must be said when all the constraints are still in place

Sleeping with you in the back of our truck
I am finally warm through.
Nothing is lost.
We don't talk of the past
but it won't go away.
We have been stretched thin
on the rack of the highway,
strung out
like laundry rinsed out
in cold washbasins
in truck-stop washrooms.
We keep our eyes at the front of our heads
and watch the sky unfold,
the road unroll;
forest and field and city and town
register in our peripheral vision.
The past follows us,
a faithful but unimaginative dog.
We don't throw it any more
of our bones.

Patricia MacDonald

Kyoto

From my window on this mountain top
I can see quite clearly the path you
took from Lake Biwa to the Imperial Palace.
A great procession with you, Lady Murasaki
being carried on a palanquin wrapped in seven
kimonos, black hair over red silk,
sweltering humidity in August as I sit here
in my slip eyeing the kimono displayed on the wall.
But you chronicled all this in your pithy
novel, the first ever written, The Tale of Genji.
The manners and mores of the 12th century Heian period in Japan.
You brought alive for me the rooms I saw
in the Imperial Palace with screens to
hide your face when you were a concubine.
Yes, there was passion and so intuned with nature
as it still is even today.   Moon viewing rooms
for parties drinking sakÈ or wheat tea.
The civility of the people exists today.
I once sat where Basho went to write
his haikus.   I also saw the room where
you wrote your magnificent novel at Lake Biwa.
My heart goes out to you Lady Murasaki.

Tanis MacDonald

Orphines

Anne of Green Gables and Little
Orphan Annie were separated at birth,
born to a mother who may have been
so addled by poverty and labour that
she missed the double blessing, and
cursed them both Anne. Perhaps their
fire-engine hair confused her, burned her,
drove her to her death. Perhaps she
couldn't bear the sparrowy chirps
from their flimsy bassinets, so spunky,
such little fighters. Perhaps she sank
through the tiled floor, linked arms
with her own ghost, leaving Red Baby One
and Red Baby Two until the nuns who ran
the orphanage christened them after
the withered apple tree, last year's tomato vine,
the saint who conceived and bore ripe fruit
after her time. You can see apples
in the girls' cheeks, tomatoes in their hair.
Not carrots; Anne broke a slate over Gilbert's head,
and right she was. Tomato girls, her and
her sister, and nobody better forget it.
She always said she was leaving this poky island
and lighting out for New York, to hook
up with her sister who swung
herself a hell of a sweet deal. If only
she could steal something faster
than a leaky rowboat, she'd cut off
her braids with a boning knife and roar
down the coast, eating the spray.
She'd put eyes back in her sister's head;
she'd tell her all about the hard cheese life
in that place where even the soil was red.

Jill Margo

Heroin(e)

"Heroin," she says, "is lovely to smoke."
She is barefoot on tiptoes,
leaning slightly towards me —
as if inviting me to stare closer
at her beauty,
its mystery.

She is wearing copper-coloured silk;
a sleeveless shirt with a Chinese collar
and a thinness that betrays small breasts, erect nipples
There are pants to match that
almost do not provide
for the length of her perfect legs.

"It's oceanic," she whispers,
          rocking
back
          and forth
on tiptoes,
          "like waves."

Wendy Morton

The Sandwomen

One must have a mind of winter
To regard the frost and the boughs
Of the pinetrees crusted with snow;
And have been cold a long time.
      Wallace Stevens, "The Snow Man"

The women of Mali come out of the darkness
bearing bowls of sand;
they clear the courtyards
until the wind blows off the Sahara
from the eastern dunes;
then they stop in the sand's glitter,
still as shadows, wrapped in black.
One must have a mind of winter

to stay. The sandwomen dream
on the mind's horizon,
with the immutable grace of gazelles;
they dream of high meadows,
cold bright oceans, foam's lace,
rain   rain.
They wait
to regard the frost and the boughs

of their winter dreams.
Sand sweeps in again.
They pick up their bowls,
move into the courtyards,
move off a distance and return
to begin, begin, begin
until the dreams begin
of pinetrees crusted with snow.

76

Caravans move
through the village, carrying salt.
The women stop, lean from the doorways,
watch the traders' eyes on them.
If the wind is still they can smell the salt
from the inland sea.
They know these winter dreams
and have been cold a long time.

Richard Olafson

To Wang Wei

On a rock at the toe
Of Boat Cove
I think of Wang Wei alone.
Walking in the open body of the earth
I hear wind whistle through willows
Like a flute, the waves rising against the stones
In sorrow.
The clouds rolling across the sky
Will soon blow away.
Wang Wei,
When the chilled autumn wind
Turned red the forests of your desolation,
With harsh winds blowing at the peak,
Did thoughts of your wife
Dying in court fall with the leaves?

There were plums in my orchard too
But the crows have eaten them.
Did you
Stand at the summit
And look at the world
Below the clouds?
Did you spend such a day as this
In your youth
Alone in autumn
Listening to the far off water birds?

P.K. Page

This Heavy Craft

The wax has melted
but the dream of flight
persists.
I, Icarus, though grounded
in my flesh
have one bright section in me
where a bird
night after starry night
while I'm asleep
unfolds its phantom wings
and practices.

Kelly Parsons

Monastery Quails

Think of them coming down
from the hills, leaving the familiar

hedgerows of their birth. They will take up
residence in the ruins. Quails will begin

to walk the Holy Isle. Let them keep the hours
to their liking. Let the quails be

brothers. Hands,
nonexistent, will be tucked inside

their feathered robes, covering
hollow bones, thin skin. Their mottled

wings, brown and still. None shall
be eaten. Let the feathers grow long

and sweep the ground. They are
worthy of veneration. Let fruits be ripe

when they eat, and each one's tiny clay bowl
be filled with millet. Let them lift

their beaks and sing *Bird.* And yes
to their cloistered afternoon

scurryings, but in the evening
slow them down, their sincere

little sandaled footsteps reflective and
easy. Let the old quails stroll

the Holy Isle by moonlight. And if
they are old, let their seeds be softened.

John Pass

Titanic

It was watching Titanic I decided
to give up poetry. It was the moment

when the lovers are struggling
in the flooded compartment or corridor
or in the stairwell having just
escaped the water for the moment
or when they are freezing at sea.

It was one of those moments you know
in a story it's your story, your love, your death
they're living, barely making it

just for the moment clinging
to the rail and the futility

and sadness washed through me, the humiliation.
I was ashamed to have given so much (everything
I could) everything of enormity or not
in my life, to have given it over

to words. Words!
When this was possible:
Big Screen Big Sound, free-

falling off the stern of the century. All around me
thirteen-year-old girls sobbing, Roses afloat
for DiCaprio, so certain
they'd never let go
were letting go. So I gave up poetry

to the shrieking steel and deep ever-ending
ice-burdened kisses. The flat quiet after
under stars. It was one of those moments.

It passed.

Barbara Colebrook Peace

Homing Pigeons

And just in case that doesn't work, they've had
their olfactory nerves severed... But after you've
done this three or four times, you can get them to
home.   Rupert Sheldrake

Woozy, in a world of constant warm,
we sit woolgathering, wings against
our dozy sides. Cubicled in fluorescent summer,
our breathing dims to autumn mould.
Though we don't know the reason,
in our brains, the cherry trees are leaking.

We've never known anything but here:
white sloping chute, white floor,
a legend of a door that leads to starlight.
We sit, are sitting, sat, have sat, will sit.
The white-coated ones watch over us,
show us slides from time to time

of senseless green. We've learned
which ones to peck to get our grain,
which ones clang a shock
throughout our cells. We haven't figured
what they want from us, unless
they're lost and hope for some idea

of how they could get home —
But we can't think about it. Not
over breakfast. Later, after lunch,
we tell ourselves that if and if and if
the letter comes, and we are free once more,
we'll stumble over somehow to the door,
folding our hearts in grace

Robert Priest

Poem for the Ancient Trees

I
am young and
I want to live
to be old
and I don't want to
outlive these trees—this forest
When my last song is gone
I want these same trees
to be singing on—newer green songs
for generations to come
so let me be old let me grow
to be ancient
to come as an elder
before these same temple-green sentinels
with my aged limbs
and still know a wonder
that will outlast me
O I want long love long life
Give me
150 years
of luck
But don't
let me
outlive
these trees

a. roberts

stained and broken

her mind
crashes
back to the radio
a familiar serenade
Chopin
keyed by Gould
his usual humming along
obscured by rain washed transmission

a right turn on red
a slight scar on right...
wrist
it bothers her that the left arm
is yet unmarked

a wrist in waiting
like birds poised for take-off
a loaded gun
a starving pod of whales

the inevitability of the possible
          right wrist
          left
a wrong turn
and the radio
on

Running In

At that certain time of day
running in to anchor
fish safely bedded
under ice blankets in the hold
their eyes would meet
accustomed
winds rising on a heaving afternoon sea

And they would dream
of growing old together
of the house he would build
of the gardens she would plant
of the grandchildren who would com
once the fish were sold

Then they would take it right there
in the skipper's seat
her legs braced against the wheelhouse windows
he between her and the wheel
setting their boat
on automatic pilot
and heading it straight home

Linda Rogers

The Identical Words for Love

Pierre Elliot Trudeau,   Alfred Wellington Purdy,
(1919-2000), *in paradisum*

"Welcome to Paradise" the young
translator said when she brought
the sweet Cuban coffee
the night we slept in the VIP
lounge at the Jose Marti Airport,
where you once sat on the same sofa,
my poet friend and the hero
of the revolution across from you,
just a handshake away,
the identical words for love
slipping through your fingers.

amor, agape — words we walk on,
pass in cemeteries,
poetry carved in stone.

Imagine arriving and taking off
reading the name of Marti,
poet of the revolution.
On the anniversary of his death,
children throw flowers in a river
slowly turning to marble.
I remember putting roses in gun barrels,
the fresh rose in your lapel,
the roses on our children's graves,
a river of flowers flowing into the warm Caribbean
where we stood in the sand remembering
you had also been there with my poet
friend, resting in stone in the land
you both held in the passionate
blue-eyed gaze of rational men.

Long ago, I dreamed I walked barefoot
through snow to the top of the world,
where you were waiting in a maison
lumiére made of melting ice.
I believed I had come to
the house of the rising sun.
In dreamtime, I expected a blessing,
and you were on your knees,
reading a holy book,
which could have been written
in Latin or Sanskrit or Hebrew,
it didn't matter, because the words
for love are identical in every language.

You looked up, your eyes the colour of
sky reflected in snow, and told me to go,
"Follow my footprints home," and I did.

Little things; a dream, a Cuban child
throwing petals into the water,
our sons singing under ice, the bride
in black, who fell from your arms
into a crack in the snow,
wearing your wedding ring
on a chain around her neck,
your daughter walking behind
your coffin, head down, her hand
briefly touching the hand of the hero
of the revolution, watching
the cracks in the stone pavement,
trying not to step on any of them.

Jay Ruzesky

Lombard Street

He says yes to the long drive knowing
there will be fights with the brother,
threats from the father,
the mother's silence and bad navigation
through complex American freeways.

Yes to Alcatraz, trolley cars,
someone he wishes he could be momentarily
skateboarding down a steep incline
toward the low and distant bay,
Chinatown, and Fisherman's Wharf.
Yes to dinner at the Hilton
with its palate-cleansing sorbets between courses.

Yes to Lombard Street, the most
twisted street in the world,
the family car climbing and
this small boy outlined in the rear window,
his balloon an empty word bubble in the frame;
some cartoon character who forgot
what he was about to say.

Yes to the evening drive
across the Golden Gate Bridge,
as the city closes its slow eye.
Yes to the next day and drive home again,
to the next year when his voice broke,
and to first sex sweet in the attic of the cabin.
Yes to doing it again in the morning,
then to the few women in his life
who taught him what he knows.
Yes to the birth of his child,
to the house and jeweled yard around it.
Yes to the dog.

And now he's well into it,
there's no turning back.
Around another hairpin climbing steadily
beyond the silence surrounding
the dog's inevitable end,
so yes even to the death of his parents and
yes to being there each time.
Yes to all the routes that sent him
corkscrewing forever up like an aria.
Yes to watching his daughter
back down the driveway
graduating high school. Then yes to
old age and to senior's discounts at Sears.
Yes to memory and forgetting,
the decline of his body,
to those who call on weekends,
and to the someone who pushes him out to the park in a wheelchair.
Yes to light and dark and closing,
and Lombard Street's hedges and red bougainvillea.

Joan Ryan

Lowtide in the Rain

Almost like crossing
On nothing but a sound
From islet to island on eel grass
With rain tinkling down

Listening, wet, to the quiet
A little past sundown
Being struck by the music
Of a soft, spring rain

Hearing so many tiny temple bells
Being sounded, so many
Fragile bamboo pipes
Being played.

Sarah Lucille Selecky

november

there i am
sprawled, giggling
on a peach coloured carpet
in 1980
wearing a dress
that fell above my knees
tied at the waist
my socks sagging
a bit around
the toes
my father's winter coat
lying like a bed
at the top of the stairs
immense and elaborate
deeply scented
dark brown
i crawl in
grow smaller
disappear there

Grant Sheppard

Dogs

I belong to seven dogs.
Dogs with culvert ribs and question marks for tongues.
Tongues: seven sets of indications
slicked affection, curled
like inverted punctuation.
Tongues their every answer:
tongues that slip from shoebox mouths
as they break pace, as they rattle their chops
like castanets, lap at potholes and scowl.
Where smells linger they form wheels
not tail to tooth but snug so dogs are spokes
and dogs are fingers and there in the middle
at the axis of noses and tongues,
and flush from the chorus of sniffing
beats my own stumpy, wagging pulse.

Karen Shklanka

Right Here

The back of his jacket reads
John Deere Maximizer Combines.
His license plate is red.
I slide up behind him, hook
my thumbs in his Wranglers say, *Take me*
into a two-step honey, dance with me
beside your big truck,
right here on the deck of the Skeena Queen.

My long legs. His cowboy boots.
Let the other passengers
hang their tongues out their windows.
Rein me in, run me
into Fulford Harbour.
Let me taste salt.

Chris Smart

Ravens Speak

In the raven night, how shall I beat my wings?
How will you know my song, when you lie
sleeping? Your head tucked under feathers.

A woman opens her mouth   and a thousand ravens
fly out   black wings at dusk   she sings

all in her mouth   swallows   lives
but the forest holds her   sticky fir cones   clinging

dripping with her manís sweat   all the years
laced by fir needles   moss   blackberry vines

forests flourish between them   giants clambering in and out
of their hearts   trunks solid and straight   yet   the womanís breath
and body

light as wind in the highest branches.   She flies
settles   scrutinizes dry land   understands

ravens speak of the devil   return as black shadows landing
in her dreams   to tell a story without rhetoric

her need   mist lifting off the ocean
drifting from her mouth   sighing   feathers

Ron Smith

The Fourth Moon of Broadway

This is the avenue I remember, straight and wide,
This is the city of trees at night, fired
from the belly busting rage and swagger that chain
brother to brother. This is the city that dwells
in the tribal power of invincible youth, the will
to walk the streets in the glow of making history
from hunger and blood, the blood of prisoner and lover alike.
I wait for those who watch the slanting rain
and seek the flesh of new bone, flowers bursting into the sky
out of the appetite of skeletons, the orange blooms of night
shucked from the fourth moon of Broadway, melons
glowing overhead in the nightmare chambers
of storefronts. This is not Damascus, though dusk burns
everlasting in the recitation of the names of our beloved.
This is the will of the deal; to host the flesh reborn
from solitude, to linger at the height of orgasm.
This is the gift I hold in moonlight, soft
and transparent, open to what the heart and body crave.
This is the avenue I remember, straight and wide.

Carol Ann Sokoloff

For Charles Lillard

You left on the quiet
like you did from that party,
we had no chance to speak
I caught the corner of your lumber jacket
crossing the portal,
should have run after you,
should have called out —
already regrets —

There is a fuzzy star
in the sky these nights,
destiny's comet
dragging its tail
past your window

You reached
as one might for a fish
in a shallow stream
and hitched a ride,
a long ride,
beyond the Interior,
beyond the North
toward a further coast,
our own crested splendours
perhaps, merely an echo
of the ranges
in that dimension.

Your words,
your words you have left.
These are not quiet,
they speak and sometimes shout —
That is your way.

Glen Sorestad

Ice Fishermen

The weak sunslants of January
find them on the snowy plain
that hides the lake below. From
the jet squeezing a line of frosting
on a robin's egg sky they are mere

specks against pristine cotton,
winter anglers fled from homes
and offices, solo or in groups
of two or three, gone to the wilds
for the day. They auger down

through the lake's stiff skin,
a foot to three feet thick,
then drop their baited hooks
to rest just off the bottom,
willing a fish to strike.

They vouch they have come
to angle, but if they leave
the lake without taking fish
they will not whine about luck.
They are seekers, all — though

what it is they've come to find
is not exactly clear to each,
nor the same for all. Perhaps it is
the being here instead of there,
freedom of wind and frigid air.

Others will insist it's time,
elusive time they've come to share,
time to peer in the watery deep,
imagine the lake's beating heart;
time to lose self in the wait.

Here on the ice, they will find
what they've come for or not.
When they depart winter mends
the augered ice and slow fish
swim through the wintry dark.

Esta Spalding

On Mrs. Barlowe's Plum Tree

Actually there were crows on the branches
of the plum tree
purple-feathered in the twilight

The Sufis say the bird that flew
to look for paradise finally found it
in a mirror

These are not plums you'd put
in the fridge leaving a note to your lover
These plums taste like lemons
Evil plums   Stepmother plums

Last time D went shopping
there were eight different kinds of pepper
on his list

Who needs eight different kinds of pepper?

The point is he does the shopping

There is no Mrs. Barlowe

The Egyptian hieroglyph for mother
is the same as the one for death
a lappet-faced vulture

That tree belongs to no one
but the crows

& even they won't eat the plums

There is no plum tree
After I dreamt it
I cut it down

Susan Stenson

Family History

1.

Mother wanted to marry a different boy
but her father disapproved,
wouldn't let him into the house.
You're better than that, he'd yell
from the chair beside the stove
and she'd play piano, his favourites,
guns and mud, flasks of whiskey.
Grandfather never liked a fly in the house.
Wife would come running
with the swatter and cloth, kill it quick.

2.

Mother cut her hair. Married my father,
a tall man who played the trumpet.
I like to imagine the other one.
How I'd look had she married Sam.

It rained the night he climbed the chair
stood in the unsure light of the dining room.
What was his song? What colour was it?
Someone untied him, carried the body
up Walton Street, washed that look off his face.

3.

Sam, come down. I don't like you
hanging above my head when I walk.
Let me shine those shoes.
It's Saturday, do you dance?
You were not invited to the wedding.
Mother has no pictures in the album.

4.

I pretend I am singing for the troops.
Grandfather is there and you and Dad.
I wear mother's dress, the one you loved,
cut above the knee, pearl buttons on the sleeve.
I kill the high notes, Sam.
My stockings are silk. I take sugar
with everything. Butter too.

Tara Timmers

The Insulation Man

The insulation man came to warm the house
While the day lay resting
And I in my purple cloth
Sit consuming frosted flakes
His stomach flowed over the belt line
And he spoke in fluent gab
About heating and parliament
My eyes became black pools of interest
Sewing shut my mouth
As he became deeply involved
In the act he was there to perform
The insulation man came to warm the house
And I was already feeling the air lose its' chill
Discarding my robe
I stood naked before him,
But he kept on talking
'Bout ministry and two inch plywood
I began to dance to his melodramatic voice
The neighbors peered at us from boarded up windows
Rumours flared
I didn't care
The insulation man warmed the house
And I danced and laughed
      Laughed and danced
To the rhythmic pouring of concrete speech

Geology Class

I search through many layers of rocks
a palette of browns, oranges, yellows
poorly arranged in terra-cotta pots.

I pick a yellowish spherical one
like choosing delicate jewelry
I feel its coldness, its moon shape
the rough roundness speaks
the past
other hands that touched it
other futures.

"Pedra," I say, and
the man sitting next to me,
oriental gnome, peaceful face,
says "No, it's a rocha."

His accent comes out
in short slow moving sentences
behind him the ceiling fan blades spin slow
slow as the clock
slow as my body in this absurd heat
everything is insignificant.

I never thought about the difference between
a stone and a rock
yellow and white skin, him
and me.

My curious eyes meet his inquisitive narrow eyes:
an experiment
like others I've done before.

With a sharp tool I scrape the hard surface
brilliant fine particles levitate like pollen
land on my pale skin
in a mosaic of yellow

then I drop one,
two, three liquid beads of acid
the bubbling reaction begins
an invasion disintegrating beauty
past
future
any insignificance
I hold in my hands.

Peter Trower

Ghostcamp

A lot of loggers hide dead in these hills
setting chokers eternally
on healed slopes above brush-choked landings
where rusting steampots
crouch sphinxlike and voiceless
and corroded snake cables
twist paralyzed among the ferns
with motion, a steel memory

In the empty camp that lies
half-ransacked at the northern mouth
of this ransacked valley,
we stand thoughtful among ruin —
ancient bull-blocks
sleep like giant turtles in the weeds —
heavy two-man power-saws
lie forever unmended in sheds

Garages full of obsolete bearings —
abandoned anvils —
blacksmiths and mechanics gone
to whatever random destiny
The gutted bunkhouse guards echoes
fled dreams of drifted men
with few dreams   the cookshack
guthammer hasn't changed for years

I have come full circle   Across
the inlet lies Misery Creek
where my brother and I watched camp
one fireseason summer two decades back
The dead camp sprawls around us
I can't speak   it's too strange
Log long enough, you're bound to stumble
across your own bootprints in the end.

Meg Walker

explaining the man with feathers for hands

A woman went walking,
plasmatic.

plasmatic? "rich with life-giving blood."
no, no, that's placenta: placental, placentic.

A woman
        went walking
        plasmatic: containing her own flow
of hemoglobe order for oxygen content

but so did every other human walking by.
what was the trick, then? why
should he care she was there?

she walked perhaps
        plasmid: absolute able
        to self-duplicate and re-grow any cell.
        plasmid: why not: replicating
windows and wings for the
streets full of flyers and
back-alley needlers
        she was a
        (or was she?) a
chromosome-dropper, speed-chopping her
cell-bits at soft points of juncture
as they fell into feather-shapes
along her blue'd elbows

(sometimes the junkies would
lick the fallen shapes and fly)

        thus, daily:

the woman went walking
            plasmid and plastic
beding scurred veins into
breathing tubes of sky-light
carrying   carrying
            carrying   carrying
fragile gene divisions
with her blood-wired thighs.

whether her hope
kept her wise or inept
            was not finally clear

but when someone, just once, stood
so-near that his arms
            both dilated, his
            veins
            birthed his hairo-inn
                                        out!!!

her pieces of plumage
chasmed hap and intent: :

      leapt: :

      grafted themselves to his
      once-failing fingers

and greened there,
extruding his hope for a cure.

Family Tree in Autumn

My sisters don't live here anymore. They moved away as soon as the beets were plowed under. Even the back porch, the chimes that kept us awake all winter, couldn't hold them to this patch of wet earth. Though my cousins stayed, hoping to find some kind of redemption. They keep looking out to the sea but the sea just looks back.

The difference between then and now is the shape of a triangle. I am speaking from memory, of the manner in which your father climbed mountains: donkey, guide, the cold wind lacing his face.

Before they left my sisters dined on what they could find beneath the sink — a bottle of muscatel, licorice allsorts.

Uncle hasn't budged an inch. Except to move among the weeds and old whiskey bottles. Rain or shine he sits in a lawn chair listening to the radio's gospel cries.

And the cousins have swollen up. Bloated cherubs, they wait in waiting rooms all over the city. Not because Jesus wants someone to talk to but because the cigarette ash has piled into years.

It's November and I lie on my stomach by an open window. After she was born my daughter also lay beneath the billy lights, mask covering her eyes. Three days old, she was more croak than song, more frog than angel.

Terence Young

Castaways

I want to tell you
I no longer hate your hands,
the way they steer me and
my mother
so close to the shore.
I wish only
you didn't have to do this,
didn't have to hold us here,
always a few feet short of disaster,
from rock walls that plummet
into the black water
beneath our hull.

For once, take us where the air is warm,
lash the wheel and come
sit on the stern. Tell us of Italy,
of hyacinths and northern villas,
of cathedrals carved out
of mountains.

Watch with us
as the wake spreads out behind,
and when we run aground,
don't worry.
It will be on the finest white sand,
and the only sound will be of horses,
their hooves slipping through the long grass
next to the sea.

We will lower ourselves over the side,
immerse our bodies and wade ashore to find
a farmhouse,
its wooden siding grey from years of salty weather.
Behind it, rows of apple trees growing
wild, and under one tree a boy,
the book he was reading
open to the page where he fell
asleep.

Rodney Zimmerman

assiniboine river lament

not quite holy river
i bring news you already know.
the buffalo are gone.
the drunkard from old corruption
traded good land
for a bad railway.
vandal died so we may live
and sad to say
hirelings have hung our prophet.

Biographies

Laurie Abel's fiction and poetry has appeared in several publications including *Grain*, *The Saanich Review* and the anthology, *Wrestling with the Angel*. She currently teaches writing and literature at Camosun College in Victoria.

Mark Asser was born in Vancouver, grew up in Quebec and now helps raise a family in Victoria.

Clive Beal sleeps on Long Beach without a tent; repairs copy machines, studies the I-ching and is an artist and poet who lives in Victoria.

Lindsay Beal is a psychology student at UVic. She gets A+'s on her essays and wants to be a writer. She works with people at Blooming Humans and is blooming as a poet.

bill bissett is the author of over 40 books including *the last photo uv th human soul*. He has read and performed around the world. He has created a written language all his own, an embodiment of Canadian and North American idioms.

Yvonne Blomer's writing has been published in journals in Japan and Canada. Most recently in *The Fiddlehead* and *The Amethyst Review*. She returned to Victoria after living in Japan for two years and is currently working on a book titled *Small Japan*. Yvonne is a poet, cyclist, teacher and travel writer.

Brian Brett is a prolific writer who cultivates his garden on Salt Spring Island where he raises sheep, peacocks, a parrot and writes. *The Colour of Bones in a Stream* was published in 1998 by Sono Nis.

Tim Brownlow reminds us how much poetry matters. Born in Dublin, Ireland he has been publishing poetry since 1960 and is represented in the *Penguin Book of Irish Verse*. Oolichan Books published his latest book, *Climbing Croagh Patrick*.

Hilary Mosher Buri's chapbook *Frau Rontgen's Hand* (Outlaw Editions, 2000) received the bp Nichol award.

Margo Button's first book *The Unhinging of Wings* won the BC Poetry Prize in 1996 and was short-listed for the Gerald Lampert prize. It played as a performance piece for three weeks in Kingston, Ontario and is now being made into a film script. Her second book, *The Shadows Fall Behind* was released in 2000.

Sara Cassidy has been published in *Grain, CV 2* and *Geist*. Her chapbook, published in the Hawthorne series, is entitled *Ultrasound for the Heart*. She is involved in artistic and social causes as well as being a full time mother to Hazel, already a poetry fan.

Karen Connelly was one of the youngest writers in Canada to win the Governor General's award for her first book, *Touch the Dragon*. Her latest book is *The Border Surrounds Us,* published by McClelland & Stewart.

Lorna Crozier has won the Governor General's Award and two Pat Lowther Awards for the best book of poetry by a Canadian woman. Her latest book of poetry, *What the Living Won't Let Go*, has recently been published by McClelland & Stewart.

Cathryn Dimock has lived in Victoria for 10 years, and loves the sea. Her poems have been published in *room of one's own, convolvulus*, and *Vintage 96*. Recently returned from a visit to Japan, Cathryn is much inspired by images of temples & shrines, bamboo groves, kimono.

Mike Doyle is a poet, critic, editor and biographer. Recent work includes: *Trout Spawning at Lardeau River* (1997) and *Where to Begin: Selected letters of Cid Corman and Mike Doyle 1967-1970* (2000).

Patrick Friesen, living in Vancouver and teaching writing at Kwantlen University College, writes poetry, drama, and texts for radio, for musical improvisation and for dance. His most recent book was *Carrying the Shadow* (Beach Holme, 1999).

Gary Geddes is well known as an editor of *15 Canadian Poets x 2* and *The Art of Short Fiction, 20th-Century Poetry and Poetics*. Gary Geddes is also an award winning poet, critic and playwright. His most recent work includes *Flying Blind* and *Sailing Home: A Journey through Time, Place and Memory* (Harper Collins). He lives in French Beach near Sooke.

Susan Gee, a former CBC writer and broadcaster, is now a professional communications director. She is also a Mocambopo prize winning poet.

William George is a UVic writing and English student from the Burrard Indian Reserve in North Vancouver. His poetry and prose are published in various anthologies and literary magazines; he draws on his native heritage in the language of his poetry.

Robert Gore's poems have been widely published in literary journals and two anthologies edited by Patrick Lane. He lives in Vancouver where he works as a librarian at Kwantlen University College and sings with the acappella group, "Pastime with Good Company."

Marlene Grand Maitre's poetry was published in the anthology *Breaking the Surface*. She was selected to attend the "Otherwords" poetry workshops at the BC Festival of the Arts in Victoria in 1999.

Martin Gray has edited the Penguin edition of "Idylls of the King" as well as having published one book and several monographs on Tennyson. After a teaching career at various universities, he has fled academia for the wider and more interesting field of poetry and is currently working on another sequence of poems. His last book was *Blues for Bird* by Ekstasis Editions. He lives and writes in Victoria.

Roy Green is a painter/poet/performance artist and professional pet portraitist. He is the founding member of the interpretive dance ensemble *The Hermaphrodite Brotherhood*. He was born in the year of the dog and enjoys eating cheese.

Joelene Heathcote is completing her MFA at UBC. Many of her poems have been published in various literary journals. Her poems also appear in the anthology *Breaking the Surface* published by Sono Nis.

Steve Heighton's most recent collection of poetry, *The Ecstasy of Skeptics* was a Governor General's Award Finalist in 1995. "Were You to Die" is from that book. He has also published three books of fiction, *Flight Paths of the Emperor, On earth as it is,* and *The Shadow Boxer.* He lives in Kingston.

Vivian Hansen found Mocambo by accident, like a unique side dish in Victoria. She is a Calgary poet; also editor of *Forum* in Calgary.

Andreas Jensen is the product of a one room country schoolhouse, Ernest Manning, W.O. Mitchell, peculiar neighbours, and Danish Lutheran parents. His body was shaped by Chinooks, god-awful weather, inadequate food, and taking bull-headed risks. His mind took its shape by a terrible desire to know, see and experience everything.

Phillip C. Kelly, according to his biography when a Mocambopo feature, po-mo iconoclast Philip Kelly ("the fan man") mercilessly performs favourite self-inflicted witty songs, stylized prose fragments and thoughtful poems. After composing this song (its original music a kind of shanty) he thought he was the two-bladed fan, but now he admits he's the four-bladed fan.

Tanya Kern grew up in a hard rock town in northern Ontario. She lives in Metchosin, BC, with her two daughters and several small animals where she practices massage therapy as a day job. She has published *The Erotics of Memory* with Ekstasis Editions.

William Knowles' poetry has been published in the anthology *Breaking the Surface* as well as the journals *Afterthoughts* and *Libido.* He lives in a dilapidated Victorian house with five bikes and works in Victoria as a bike courier.

Beth Kope has been writing for decades but is just beginning to let her poetic voice speak out loud. She writes about loss, grief, abandonment, bad mothers and pigs. Her poems appear in three Outlaw Editions anthologies: *Conception, Community of Monsters* and *Blindfolds*, edited by Patrick Lane.

Timothy Stuart Lander is well known around the Pacific Northwest for his bardic West Coast lyrical long beard poems. A resident of Nanaimo, Tim is constantly travelling to where people talk about and perform poetry. He reads his poetry superbly.

Patrick Lane has published twenty-seven books of poetry and fiction over the past forty years. He lives in Victoria with his companion, Lorna Crozier and teaches widely. He has won every literary prize in Canada and is considered by most writers and critics to be one of the finest poets of his generation. His most recent book is *The Bare Plum of Winter Rain.*

Mark Lindenberg is a freelance writer, published poet and social worker who happens to have a disability. He lives in Victoria, B.C.

Tim Lilburn has published 5 books of poetry, been nominated for the Governor General's Award. His latest book is *To the River.*

Susan E. McCaslin is an instructor of English at Douglas College in Coquitlam, B.C. and the author of eight volumes of poetry. Her most recent titles are: *The Altering Eye* (Borealis Press, 2000) and *Flying Wounded* (University Press of Florida, 2000). She lives in Port Moody, BC with her husband and daughter.

Wendy McGrath's prize winning poems have been broadcast on the CBC. Her first book is *Common Place Ecstasies*, published by Beach Holme.

Paddy McCallum's poem, "The Pioneer Graveyard at Nicola Lake," was published in his first book *Parable Beach* by Beach Holme in 2000. A second, *From Where The Trees Are Standing In The Water* will be published in the spring of 2002. He was the winner of the Arc Millennium Poetry Prize in 2000 and lives in Gibsons, B.C.

Leanne McIntosh lives in Nanaimo, B.C. Her poems have been published in *Grain*, *The Malahat Review*, *Event*, several anthologies and chapbooks. She is currently working on a manuscript titled, *The Sound the Sun Makes*.

Don McKay's latest books are *Night Field*, *Apparatus* and *Another Gravity* (2000). He has lived in central Canada, the Maritimes and BC, where he currently makes his home.

Andrea McKenzie was born in Smithers, B.C. and has lived in Victoria ever since. A graduated English major from the University of Victoria she was a featured poet at Mocambo Café in February 1999 and hopes to eventually achieve the task of being published. She writes poems about train rides, and love in New Zealand, New York & Wal-Mart.

Chris McPherson is a hypnotherapist who lives in Victoria. He is author of the short story collections *Everything but the Truth* and *Dragons,* a short dark novel about light. He wrote this poem while on book tour with his life-partner, Carolyn. He loves her more than anything.

Patricia MacDonald dressed up when she came to Mocambopo, wore sequins and hats. She loved to hear the readers and sometimes got up at the open mike and delighted us all. She died in Naples, Spring 2001.

Tanis MacDonald's first book of poetry, *Holding Ground* (Seraphim Editions) was published in 2000 and nominated for Manitoba's Eileen McTavish Sykes Award, and the League of Canadian Poets' Gerald Lampert Award for best first book of poetry. She won the Milton Acorn-Muriel Rukeyser Award in 1997. Originally from Winnipeg, Tanis is a doctoral candidate in English at UVic.

Unable to pursue a career as a wet nurse to wild animals, **Jill Margo** is instead a poet, writer and publisher. She is the author of the chapbook *Soft Burning*, by Fine Words Chapbooks. She resides in Fairfield with her special man-friend and a hairless cat.

Wendy Morton is the current host of Mocambopo. She has just published her first book of poetry with Ekstasis Editions titled *Private Eye*.

She always carries a few poems with her in the case of an emergency, and once was stopped for speeding, pulled out a poem and read her way out of a ticket.

Richard Olafson, publisher of Ekstasis Editions most recently read from *Roses. Pearls. Ocean. Stars. Triads* in a 1000 year old monastery in Paris. "Language breaks on a stone of silence, waves form."

PK Page lives in Victoria, B.C.

Kelly Parsons was one of six new poets in *Threshold* (Sono Nis, 1998) and her poetry and reviews have recently appeared in *The Malahat Review*. She lives in Victoria.

John Pass's poetry has been published widely in Canada since the 1970's. His thirteenth collection *Water Stair* (Oolichan Books, 2000) was nominated for a Governor General's Award. He lives on BC's Sunshine Coast with his wife, writer Theresa Kishkan, and their three children.

Barbara Colebrook Peace's first book of poems, *Kyrie*, was published in spring 2001 by Sono Nis Press.

Robert Priest is a Poet, Songwriter, Playwright and Novelist. Robert Priest is one of the few artists who has made a mark for himself in both the musical and literary fields. As a musician he has worked with Alannis Morrisette, Alanna Myles and Tom Cochrane and formed various bands. He has released children's songs with the children's rock group, The Teds and written a number of children's books. He has published numerous books of poetry, a novel, and had his plays professionally produced. He has recently published a book of poems, *Resurrection in the Cartoon* (ECW), and EMI has recently released his popular CD, *Tongue 'N Groove*. His latest book for children, *The Secret Invasion of Bananas*, will be released this fall from Ekstasis.

a. roberts is a seamstress with the whitest fingers and the blackest thread. If uranium could speak, she would translate.

Dorothy Rogers was born on the island of Malta. She is an ex-commercial fish slave, an ex-tree-planter, mother of one, a sometime traveler, perennial bon vivante and a complete fool for love. She is presently a graduate student at Uvic, where she is counting the days.

Linda Rogers is a poet and a fiction writer living in Victoria, B.C. Currently the people's poet for Canada, she was recently in Cuba in the room where her two friends, one a poet, the other a politician, met Fidel Castro years ago.

Jay Ruzesky's poems and stories have appeared in Canadian and American journals. His books include *Writing on the Wall* (Outlaw Editions, 1996). He is on the editorial board of the Malahat Review and teaches at Malaspina University-College.

Joan Ryan is a decorative artist and descriptive writer who lives close to the beach in her native Victoria.

Sarah Lucille Selecky lives, writes and paints in Victoria. Her poems and stories have been published in *The Peterborough Review*, *Hydrate*, *Island Words* and *Fire and Reason*.

Grant Shepard used to teach in Bella Bella. Then he decided he wanted to be a writer. He is now in his third year in the Creative Writing Department at the University of Victoria and is currently waiting for significant cosmic instruction.

Karen Schlanka's poetry has been published in three chapbooks edited by Patrick Lane, and in *Prism* International. She attended the 1997 B.C. Festival of the Arts. She is a family physician on Saltspring Island.

Chris Smart is a public health nurse on Salt Spring, a runner, a poet.

Ron Smith is the author of three books of poetry *Seasonal*, *A Buddha Named Baudelaire* and *Enchantment & Other Demons* and a collection of short stories, *What Men Know About Women*. His writing has appeared in magazines and anthologies in Australia, Canada, England, Italy, Yugoslavia and the States. He lives in Lantzville on Vancouver

Island and is currently working on a novel.

Carol Ann Sokoloff has published four books including *Eternal Lake O'Hara* and *A Light Unbroken* (poetry); *New Sufi Songs and Dances* (metaphysics); and a recent illustrated children's book *Colours Everywhere you Go* (with artist Tineke Visser). A native of Toronto, she is also a songwriter, performer and middle eastern dance instructor as well as editor for Ekstasis Editions and parent of two great boys with poet-publisher Richard Olafson in Victoria, BC.

Glen Sorestad is Saskatchewan's first Poet Laureate. His recent poetry books include *Icons of Flesh* (1998), *Today I Belong to Agnes* (2000) and *Leaving Holds Me Here* (2001).

Esta Spalding is the author of three books of poetry: *Carrying Place, Anchoress*, and *Lost August*. "On Mrs. Barlowe's Plum Tree" is from her forthcoming collection *The Wife's Account*. She lives in Vancouver where she writes for film and television.

Susan Stenson teaches English and creative writing in Victoria. Her first book of poems, *Could Love a Man* (Sono Nis Press) was released spring 2001. She loves her husband and kids first, poetry second.

Tara Timmers once showed us how poetry effected her and pointed to her heart. We wanted her to read more at Mocambopo, but she disappeared.

Renata Tobias was born in Brazil and immigrated to Canada in 1996, where she discovered her passion for writing. She now lives in Liberty Lake, Washington, USA with her husband and two sons. She's going to study Electronic Media and Film at Eastern Washington University next fall.

Peter Trower began writing seriously in the late 1950's after an abortive fling at professional cartooning. He published his first collection of poetry in 1969. In 1971 he quiet logging and went to work at *Raincoast Chronicles* as the Associate Editor. His recent work includes *Chainsaws* *in the Cathedral* (Ekstasis 1999), *A Ship Called Destiny: Yvonne's Book* (Ekstasis 2000) and *The Judas Hills* (2000).

Meg Walker wanders the world with Don Quixote, Emily Dickinson and other voices in her head, painting when she's in one place and scribbling on rocks when she's in transit. Calender girl for Victoria's *Monday* Magazine. Chagrined to be monolingual. Practicing drowning lit theory in the sea.

Patricia Young has published 7 books of poetry, won a bushel basket full of awards, including the Pat Lowther Memorial Prize, the BC Book Prize, and the League of Canadian Poets National competition. Her latest book, *What I remember from my time on earth*, is published by Anansi. She was a finalist for the Governor General's Award for poetry for her book, *More Watery Still*.

Terence Young's first collection of poetry, *The Island in Winter*, was nominated in 1999 for the Governor General's award. His first book of fiction, *Rhymes With Useless*, will be published by Raincoast Books this year.

Rodney D. Zimmerman is a neopostmodern poet enamored with the classics whose work focuses on images of the human experience in order to deliver an entertaining and thought-provoking story. You may have heard Rod before at Mocombopo's open mike reciting "Dancing with my Ignorance," "Be" (that's B single E) and "The Raid on Dieppe."